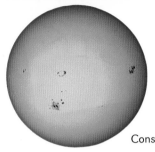

These content vocabulary word builders
are for grades 1–2.

Consultant: Michelle Yehling, Astronomy Education Consultant

Photo Credits:

Photographs © 2008: Corbis Images: 1, 5 bottom left, 7 (Paul A. Souders), 4 top, 5 top right, 16, 17 (Craig Tuttle); Getty Images/Doug Armand: 4 bottom right, 9; Holiday Film Corp.: back cover; NASA: cover; Photo Researchers, NY: 2, 5 top left, 13 (John Chumack), 19 (Gregory G. Dimijian), 5 bottom right, 15 (Scharmer et al, Royal Swedish Academy of Sciences), 4 bottom left, 11 (Detlev van Ravenswaay); Tom Stack & Associates, Inc.: 23 (NOAA/TSADO).

Illustration Credit:

Illustration pages 20–21 by Greg Harris

Book Design: Simonsays Design!
Book Production: The Design Lab

Library of Congress Cataloging-in-Publication Data
Chrismer, Melanie.
The sun / by Melanie Chrismer.—Updated ed.
   p. cm.—(Scholastic news nonfiction readers)
Includes bibliographical references and index.
ISBN-13: 978-0-531-14753-5 (lib. bdg.)   978-0-531-14768-9 (pbk.)
ISBN-10: 0-531-14753-3 (lib. bdg.)   0-531-14768-1 (pbk.)
1. Sun—Juvenile literature. I. Title.
QB521.5.C57 2007
523.7—dc22   2006102775

16 17 18 R 21 20 19 18 17

SCHOLASTIC
News
Nonfiction Readers

UPDATED
The Sun

By Melanie Chrismer

CONTENTS

WORD HUNT

Look for these words as you read. They will be in **bold**.

atmosphere
(**at**-muhss-fihr)

solar system
(**soh**-lur **siss**-tuhm)

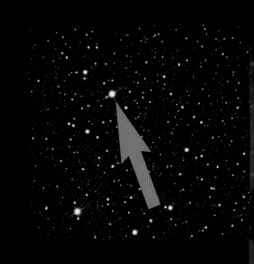

star
(star)

4

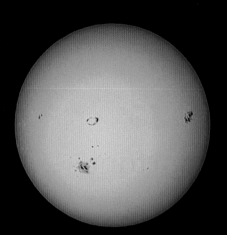

photosphere
(**foh**-toh-sfihr)

radiation
(ray-dee-**ay**-shuhn)

Sun
(suhn)

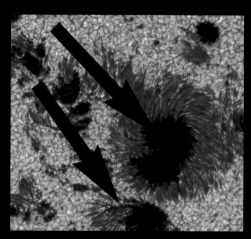

sunspots
(**suhn**-spots)

5

The Sun!

The **Sun** is very important to us.

It gives us light and heat. We need the Sun to live.

Can you visit the Sun?

No. Let's see why.

The Sun comes up, or rises, in the east.
It goes down, or sets, in the west.

The Sun is a **star**.

Stars are big balls of hot gas.

The Sun looks bigger than other stars.

It is not. It is just closer to us. Other stars are much farther away.

star

Stars look small because they are far away.

The Sun is the biggest object in our **solar system**.

Most of the other objects in our solar system travel around the Sun.

The planets are small next to the Sun.

Sun

Earth

The Sun is very hot.

The Sun's surface is about 10,000 degrees!

The surface of the sun is called the **photosphere**.

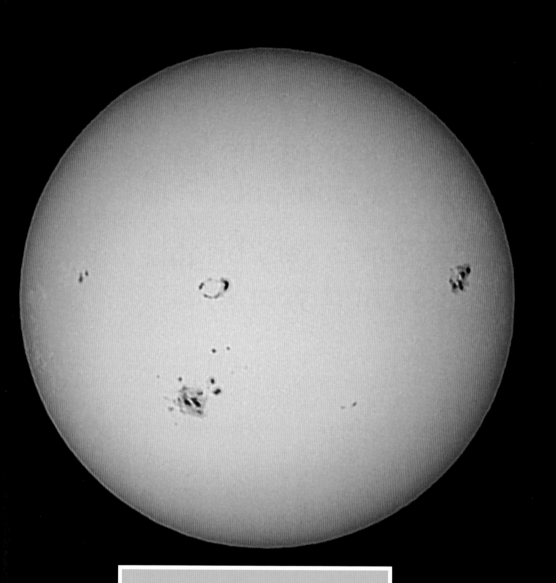

This is the surface of the Sun.

The photosphere has dark areas called **sunspots**.

Never look at the Sun to hunt for sunspots.

The Sun is very bright. It can hurt your eyes.

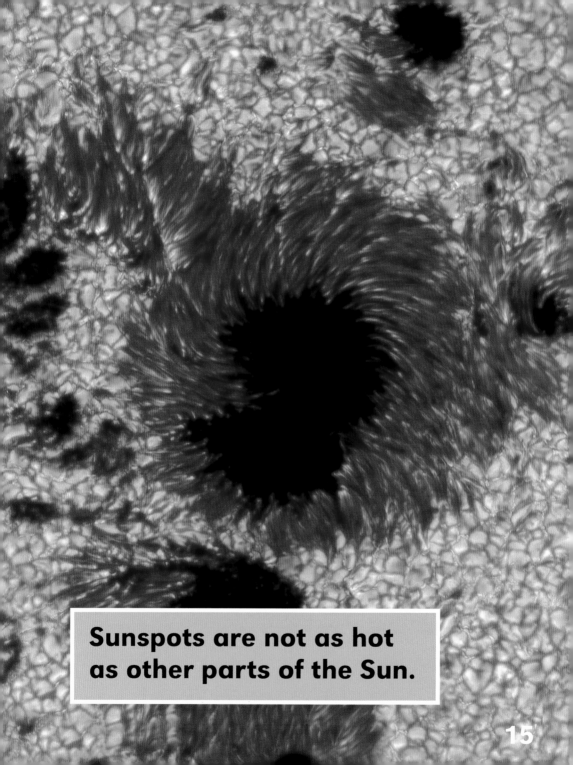

Sunspots are not as hot as other parts of the Sun.

The Sun gives Earth light and heat called **radiation**.

The Sun can warm up a place even if it is cold.

Earth's blue sky comes from sunlight shining through our **atmosphere**.

radiation

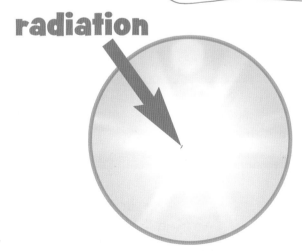

atmosphere

The Sun is too hot and too bright to visit.

It is 93 million miles away from Earth.

That is very far away, but it is just right for life on Earth!

Life on Earth depends on the Sun.

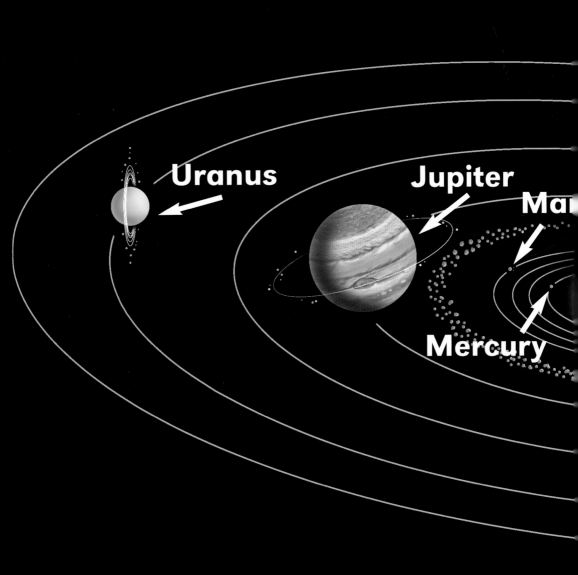

Uranus

Jupiter

Ma[

Mercury

THE SUN

IN OUR SOLAR SYSTEM

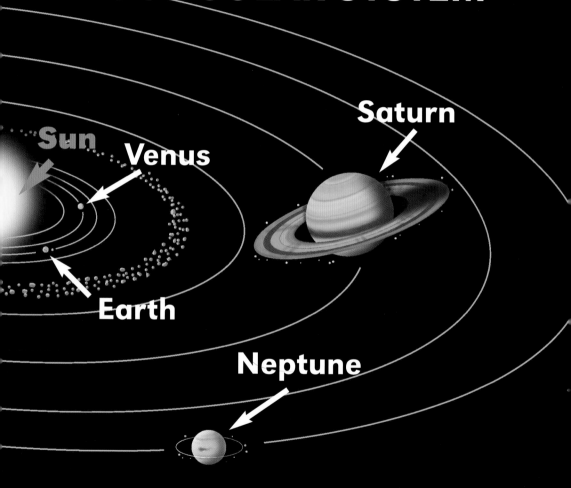

Saturn

Sun

Venus

Earth

Neptune

YOUR NEW WORDS

atmosphere (**at**-muhss-fihr) the gas around a planet

photosphere (**foh**-toh-sfihr) the surface of the Sun

radiation (ray-dee-**ay**-shuhn) waves of energy and light

solar system (**soh**-lur **siss**-tuhm) the group of planets, moons, and other things that travel around the Sun

star (star) a ball of hot gas that gives off light and heat

Sun (suhn) the biggest object in our solar system

sunspots (**suhn**-spots) dark areas on the surface of the Sun

The Sun Is an Amazing Star!

It takes about 600 hours for the Sun to turn one time. This is about 25 days on Earth.

The Sun is about 5 billion years old.

The Sun is a star, not a planet.

More than 1 million Earths could fit inside the Sun.

INDEX

FIND OUT MORE

Book:

Cole, Michael D. *The Sun: Center of the Solar System.* Berkeley Heights, NJ: Enslow Publishers, Inc., 2001.

Web site:

Sun Information and Pictures
*http://starchild.gsfc.nasa.gov/docs/StarChild/
solar_system_level1/sun.html*

MEET THE AUTHOR

Melanie Chrismer grew up near NASA in Houston, Texas. She loves math and science and has written thirteen books for children. To write her books, she visited NASA where she floated in the zero-gravity trainer called the Vomit Comet. She says, "it is the best roller coaster ever!"

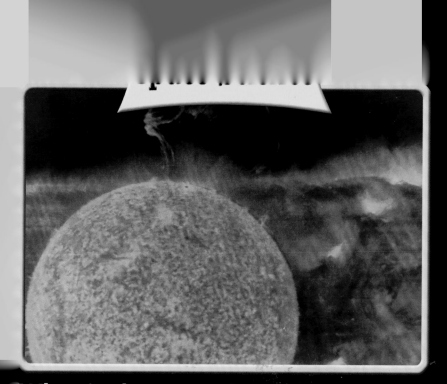

What is the Sun? The Sun is a star.
Stars are big balls of hot gas.
Can you visit the Sun?

Let's find out! Look inside to learn
more about the Sun and its place
in space!

U.S. $6.95

ldren's press®

an imprint of

SCHOLASTIC

olastic.com/librarypublishing

Guided Reading Level: I
Word Count: 205
Decodability: 70%
Sight Words: 36

ISBN-13: 978-0-531-14
ISBN-10: 0-531-14768-

9 780531 147689